A Dictionary of

Polspeak

What Politicians Really Mean

by

Hal Lillywhite

What Politicians Really Mean
A Dictionary of Polspeak

Introduction

Do you think your representative or senator speaks English? Nope. What he speaks has only a superficial similarity to English. If you want to understand politicians you need to know something about their language.

Words and phrases can have different meanings in different languages. For example, "rat" in English means a rodent that most people don't like. However in German it means "council," hence the German word for city hall is "Rathaus." (Pronunciation very similar to "rat house," make of that what you will.) If we are to understand the Germans we must know what the words mean as the Germans use them.

Likewise politicians. To understand politicians we must know what the words mean when politicians use them. That means we must study their language. Most politicians and many government officials speak *Polspeak*. Some journalists and academics also use Polspeak. The Polspeak language is easily mistaken for English since it uses the same words and phrases as does English. However in Polspeak those words and phrases do not mean what they would mean in English. In fact, much like English, a word in Polspeak can have more than one meaning, depending on the context and who is speaking. And much like English, the meaning of a Polspeak word can change with time and place. Adding to the confusion, in Polspeak that meaning tends to change even faster than in English.

F. A. Hayek in his book, *The Road to Serfdom,* describes the ill effects of this changing of word meaning. "...it is difficult to appreciate the magnitude of this change of meaning of words, the confusion which it causes, and the barriers to any rational discussion which it creates. It has to be seen to be understood how, if one of two brothers embraces the new faith, after a short while he appears to speak a different language which makes any real communication between them impossible. And the confusion becomes worse because this change of meaning of the words describing political ideals is not a single event but a continuous process, a technique employed consciously or unconsciously to direct the people. Gradually, as this process continues, the whole language becomes despoiled, and words become empty shells deprived of any definite meaning, as capable of denoting one thing as its opposite and used solely for the emotional associations which still adhere to them."[1]

This dictionary is intended to promote understanding between citizens and their hired help in political office. It presents commonly misunderstood words and phrases, together with their meanings in English and in Polspeak. Whenever dealing with politicians or government officials, citizens are urged to remember what the words mean in Polspeak. That will help them understand what the speaker really means.

[1] F. A. Hayek, *The Road to Serfdom, the Definitive Edition,* University of Chicago Press, 2007, p175. Note that this book has been printed in more than one format and pagination may vary with printing. The quote is found in Chapter 11.

Polspeak Dictionary

Access

English: An opening or other means whereby people can, of their own volition and by their own effort, enter some edifice or area. For example, stairs leading to a second floor provide access to that floor.

Polspeak: Giving people something, usually at no cost to the recipient. For example giving them employment. However in Polspeak this word is usually used in the negative and blamed on others. A young person who goofs off in school and fails to acquire employment skills will be said to have been denied access to a good job. A person who spent his money on vacations, concerts, a fancy TV etc. instead of health insurance is said to have been denied access to health care.

Achievement

English: An accomplishment by some individual or group, either a government or private entity. For example it is an accomplishment when a person creates a successful business, or when a piano student masters a difficult piece.

Polspeak: Something government does, such as pass a law or write a regulation. It is considered an achievement regardless of whether that law accomplishes its alleged purpose. For example it is an achievement that there are de facto quotas in hiring. However in Polspeak, non-government accomplishments are not achievements, they are the result of privilege.

Action

English: Doing something beyond talking. For example, locking up criminals so they cannot commit more crimes, or expanding road capacity in congested areas.

Polspeak definition 1: Making and publicizing plans to fix a problem, especially when accompanied by large expenditures involved in such planning. For example, spending a lot of money and getting a lot of attention in the news for making plans to replace an aging bridge.

Polspeak definition 2: Throwing lots of money or regulation at the problem.

Affirmative Action

English: Acting to solve a problem. For example, training the unskilled to do certain jobs so that they become employable. Another example would be improving education in inner cities so children from those areas have a chance at good employment.

Polspeak: A de facto quota system. Discriminating in employment, such as hiring or promoting a woman or minority, even when a more qualified non-minority person is available.

Ask

English: Making a request and letting the person asked either agree to the request or refuse that request. For example asking a neighbor to help move furniture in a house.

Polspeak: Forcing citizens to do something. For example, "asking" that people pay more taxes, then if they refuse either garnishing their bank accounts or putting them in jail.

Bigot

English: Someone who hates or discriminates against those of other races, sexual orientation, or sex. For example the Ku Klux Klan, or the employer who refuses to hire a black person.

Polspeak definition 1: Any political conservative.

Polspeak definition 2: Anyone who objects to participation in affirmative action as described in the Polspeak definition of that term.

Polspeak definition 3: Anyone who does not support a government proposal.

Polspeak definition 4: Anyone who opposes a black politician or what that politician does, regardless of the reason for that opposition. For example someone who opposes Barack Obama's efforts to take over the health care system. However in order to be considered bigotry, that black politician must meet the requirements in definition 1 of Polspeak for a Black Man/Woman

Black Man/Woman

English: A person of African descent with dark skin. For example Clarence Thomas.

Polspeak definition 1: A person of at least partly African descent who supports big government and votes democratic. In Polspeak, Clarence Thomas is not an authentic black man because he is politically conservative.

(Continued on the next page)

Black Man/Woman (Continued)

Polspeak definition 2: A person with any significant black ancestry, even maybe an eighth black This definition comes from the south in the days of slavery and Jim Crow when bigots needed it to discriminate. However it is still used by some, especially on the left. Those people often want to use government power to confer special benefits on the people they call black (and buy their votes).

Budgeting

English: Making certain that expenditures are applied to the highest priorities and do not exceed available resources. For example, if a company expects a billion dollars to be available, its management will make sure that its expenditures are no more than that amount. The wise management team will then fund top priorities such as building and equipment maintenance first and only build that fancy recreation center for employees if there is money left over to do it.

Polspeak: Funding preferred (pork barrel) projects before the funding of critical government functions such as education or public safety. That helps create a requirement for more taxes or borrowing to meet urgent needs. For example, at the beginning of a session, a legislature may fund favored art projects, government buildings, or new roads in the districts of powerful representatives. Then, as the session approaches its end, they will discover the need for more tax money to fund public safety, education and repair of some critical bridges.

Censorship

English: Using the force of law to prevent expression of certain ideas, publication of certain books etc. For example blocking publication of a book or newspaper article critical of the government.

Polspeak: Failure to use tax money to pay an artist or buy a particular book for the library. For example, not using tax money to hire an artist who wants to paint a work that offends most people.

Charity

English: Voluntary giving of money, time, or other resources to help the less fortunate. For example, giving money to the Red Cross or Salvation Army, or donating time to work on projects such as park improvement or tutoring school children.

Polspeak: Using government force to take money from taxpayers for the supposed benefit of the less fortunate. For example, providing tax-funded cell phones to those who say they are poor.

Choice

English: The ability to decide for oneself in most aspects of life. For example, deciding what you will eat, where your children will go to school, where you will go on vacation, etc. People who support school vouchers are supporting choice since they want to allow parents the choice of which school their children attend.

Polspeak: Abortion.

Communicate

English: A Clear, two-way transfer of information, desires, needs etc. so that both parties understand what is being communicated. For example, making sure that your children understand exactly which TV shows they are allowed to watch, or what time they should be home from a date.

Polspeak: Leading people to believe one thing while really trying to do something else. For example, saying that you are a fiscal conservative, then supporting new spending measures or defending wasteful expenditures. Use of "weasel words," euphemisms etc. is very helpful.

Correct

English: That which is correct, does not harm others etc. For example a correct action would be to drive carefully and legally.

Polspeak: Whatever a judge or bureaucrat decides is or should have been the correct action. For example, a student on a college campus must express only politically correct opinions. If he says something negative about affirmative action (as defined for Polspeak), the college authorities can decide it was offensive and punish him. The student's right or correct action would have been to not make the negative statement, even if the rules were unclear when he spoke.

Criminal

English: Someone who violates the law, especially by committing a felony such as theft or murder. For example, people who engage in mass shootings.

Polspeak definition 1: There is no such thing as a criminal. There are only misunderstood and mistreated people who must do what they do because of how society has treated them, or there are people who are accused of violence that is really the fault of inanimate objects. Shootings at schools or other public places are really the fault of the gun and of society for giving the shooter a reason to kill people and allowing access to a gun.

Polspeak definition 2: Anyone who opposes a law or regulation the speaker regards as important. For example, opponents of the law called Obamacare.

Code Words

English: Words the speaker uses to hide true meaning. For example "spending reduction" used to mask an actual increase in government spending. (See the definition for spending reduction.) In fact much of the Polspeak vocabulary consists of code words.

Polspeak: Any word spoken by a political conservative that can be twisted to imply racism, regardless of what the speaker means. For example, the word "Chicago" is called a code word and claimed to be a racist reference to Blacks if a conservative mentions that Barack Obama is from Chicago. There is an essentially complete list of what the left will call code words. It is called the *Oxford English Dictionary*.

Compromise

English: Each side gives up something it wants to reach an agreement both can live with.

Polspeak definition 1: I keep accusing you of refusal to compromise until I get everything I want. What you get out of it is that I stop making those accusations – until the next time we disagree.

Polspeak definition 2: Making lots of noise about how you are fighting for what you believe in, then giving up pretty much everything while claiming that you got the best deal possible.

Constitutional Interpretation

English: Seeking the meaning of the constitution as it was written. That is likely to include trying to determine the meaning of the words as those words were used when the document was created.

Polspeak: Finding a way to make it appear that the constitution supports what you want to do anyway.

Conservative

English definition 1: Someone who does not like change in any form. For example someone who opposed the introduction of cell phones because it would require him to learn something new, or because he feared unknown consequences of that technology.

English definition 2: A risk adverse person, someone who is very careful in life. For example an investor who buys nothing but AAA rated bonds, or a parent who refuses to allow his or her children to play sports because of the risk of injury.

Polspeak: Anyone who opposes an increase in government power or who wants to reduce that power. In Polspeak, resistance to change is irrelevant since many "conservatives" do want changes such as reduction in government, or more effective education. However since those people resist big government they are called conservatives in Polspeak.

Crisis

English: A sudden event or series of events that is likely to cause major problems in the life of one or more people. One example would be an earthquake or a major disease epidemic. To be a crisis an event must be severe and either sudden or worsening.

Polspeak: Any problem, inconvenience or situation that can be made to appear threatening. This need not be a new or worsening problem, it is only necessary that it be possible to make it appear bad. For example, you might find that there are still poor people in the country, or at least people who can be defined as poor. Even if poverty has been declining, you can call this a crisis and use it to frighten people into voting as you want them to vote. Hence the statement by some in politics, "Never let a good crisis go to waste." They know that they can use a crisis, real or manufactured, to panic people into supporting measures that increase their power. Then the important aspect of the proposed solution is creating the impression of progress. Actually solving the problem is not necessary and often counterproductive. Should the problem cease to exist the politician will lose the excuse for the increased power that the "solution" gives him.

Discrimination

English: Hiring, firing, promoting etc. on the basis of skin color or sex.

Polspeak: Insisting on hiring the best person for the job and failing to meet de facto quotas of women or minorities. This is in fact the opposite of the English definition of the word.

Diversity

English: A range of people of different characteristics. This may include "liberals," "conservatives," the black and white, those of differing experiences etc. This type of diversity is useful to get a range of opinions thus improving decision making.

Polspeak: Having the required percentages of different skin colors and sexes. Differing political opinions or experiences do not count.

Education

English: Teaching students valuable skills and knowledge. That would include reading, writing, mathematics, science, accurate history etc. It might also include teaching critical thinking. The important point is that the students must learn something significant. If they do not learn, education has not occurred.

Polspeak definition 1: Having students sit in class the requisite number of hours per week.

Polspeak definition 2: Providing money to school employees.

Polspeak definition 3: Getting students to accept the prevailing political viewpoint. Critical thinking of course is not allowed, the students might begin thinking clearly about such things as the promises politicians make.

Emotional Issue

English: Any issue on which people act based solely or mostly on emotion rather than thinking it out. For example unthinking opposition to having a black person as a neighbor.

Polspeak: Anything important to the opposition and which your side does not like. For example those who believe in few limits on government power would say that limited government is an emotional issue, regardless of the thinking behind that desire to limit government power.

Enlightenment

English: Learning something important or overcoming a false belief. For example, becoming aware of the "gamblers' fallacy" and changing how one lives accordingly.

Polspeak: Joining our side.

Entitlement

English: Something you have earned by your work or paid for with your money. For example the salary from your job, or the retirement money you earned and saved.

Polspeak: Anything politicians can use to buy your vote while telling you that you deserve it. For example, medical treatment for things like erectile dysfunction for those who cannot or do not want to pay for it themselves.

Equality

English: Treating everyone alike, subject only to differences in attitude, talent, etc. Usually understood to mean that everyone should have an equal opportunity, though those with more talent and diligence will naturally excel.

Polspeak: Equal outcome regardless of talent or diligence. If a woman or minority does not reach the same employment level as a white man, that is prima facie evidence of inequality and discrimination. Ability and diligence matter little or not at all for this definition.

Equal Employment Opportunity

English: The company hires or promotes whoever appears to be the best person for the job. This is based solely on job-related qualifications and ignores irrelevancies like skin color. It follows Martin Luther King's desire that people should be judged by the content of their character rather than the color of their skin. Equal opportunity requires that employment decisions be made solely on the basis of the value an employee brings to the company.

Polspeak: The company will hire and promote the right statistical balance, even if it has to give preference to people of one sex or skin color. Group identity must trump qualifications and value to the company.

Excluded

English: Deliberately keep out of something, such as a person not allowed to join the country club because he is black.

Polspeak: Not given some opportunity, regardless of the reason. For example if a person fails to develop skills for a job, we say that the company excluded him from that employment.

Feasible

English: Can be accomplished at reasonable expenditure of money, time, and effort. For example, it is feasible to expect students to learn and to grade them on what they learn. We know it is feasible since it has been done for centuries.

Polspeak: What? Never heard of such a thing! If we want to do something we should do it, regardless of cost. Anyone who opposes our proposal is just an obstructionist.

Free Speech

English: The right to say what you want to say or what you believe in, so long as it does not actually harm others. For example you can say bad things about the president but you may not yell "fire" in a crowded theater (unless there really is a fire there). Any restrictions on speech must be very limited and determined by the illegal action of a speaker. Urging people to riot can be prohibited, but speaking ill of someone is legal, even if listeners go too far with their objections. Speech that offends someone is still protected since there is no right not to be offended. However the right to speak does not include the right to be taken seriously or to be paid for your opinions.

Polspeak definition 1: The right to say what you believe as long as it does not offend protected groups such as homosexuals, minorities, or Muslims. In Polspeak, it is the offended person who decides if the speech is offensive.

Polspeak definition 2: The right to have your speech broadcast to an audience, by subsidized media if necessary; for example the right to be on public access television. However this right does not extend to speech deemed offensive by the authorities, such as broadcasting opinions against things like "affirmative action."

Freedom

English: The right to make decisions for yourself provided you have the means and ability to do what you want, and that it is not illegal. The person making the choice then accepts both the good and bad consequences of that choice. For example, the right to decide on your own career if you are good enough at it to make a living. Another example would be the right to buy and consume food you like, regardless of whether government considers that food to be good for you or not. Of course that includes accepting the effects of eating that food.

Polspeak definition 1: The right to force someone else to provide you with the means to do what you want. In Polspeak, a person is not free to decide on a career unless he is guaranteed a living from that career, at taxpayer expense if necessary. An artist is not free unless he is guaranteed payment for his work, regardless of whether or not customers want to pay for that work. However in Polspeak, freedom does not include the right to do something like eat an unhealthy meal.

Polspeak definition 2: The right to do what you want without fear of consequences. For example the right to goof off in school or study a field with poor job prospects, then demand that government (that is, the more diligent people who pay taxes) support you.

Gay

English: Happy, carefree. For example a children's party in which all the children laugh, play and generally enjoy themselves. In English, the word has no sexual connotations.

Polspeak: Homosexual. (The Polspeak folks and homosexuals have taken over this word to the point that it has essentially lost its true meaning.)

Goal (also sometimes called a Target)

English: Something nice to reach but with no legal consequences if an organization does not meet the goal. For example a business might have a goal to promote a certain number of its minority employees and might provide them extra training to try to reach that goal. However should that training not prepare the employees for promotion, there are no legal consequences.

Polspeak: A numerical target of minority or female hiring or promotion that must be met. If it is not met, legal action will follow. Of course this is not a quota; it is just a goal with legal consequences.

Greed

English: The desire to acquire more and more money, power, land etc. This applies to everybody, private citizens, companies, and government officials. In fact greed is part of normal human makeup and affects essentially the entire human race, and even many animals.

Polspeak: The desire to acquire more and more money, power, land etc. This applies to private citizens and businesses but in Polspeak does not apply to government, or to rich supporters of big government such as Warren Buffet or George Soros.

Harassment

English: Talk or action that deliberately bothers someone. Examples would be vandalizing the target's car or home, threatening bodily harm or property damage, continuing to contact the target after a request to desist, etc. The man who continues to pursue a woman after being asked to leave her alone, or the person who throws garbage in a neighbor's yard would be guilty of harassment. In English harassment is determined by the actions of the harasser.

Polspeak: Anything the supposed target deems offensive. For example, a man might tell a woman that she is pretty. If she likes it he has not committed harassment. However if she does not like it or just wants to harm him, she can decide it is harassment. In Polspeak, harassment is determined by the reaction of the victim.

Hate/Hate Speech

English: Hatred or saying undeserved bad things about a person or group. For example claiming that all Blacks or Mexicans are thieves and should be hung. Lumping everyone in a group together.

Polspeak definition 1: Anything not positive about any protected group or certain politicians. For example, pointing out that inner city gangs in some places are mostly black. Truth does not matter here.

Polspeak definition 2: Opposing the politics of minority politicians, regardless of the reasons for that opposition. For example opposing President Obama's health care law is called hate speech, even if the person opposing has nothing against Blacks but just does not believe in government controlled health care.

Homophobia

English: Fear of homosexuals, for example refusing to speak to or have contact with known homosexuals. To be a phobia this must include actual fear.

Polspeak: Failing to fully support what the homosexual community wants. For example opposing homosexual marriage, regardless of the reasons for such opposition. Actual fear is not necessary to this definition.

Immigrant

English: A foreigner who enters the country with the proper approval and the intent to remain permanently. Such approval normally includes a passport and immigrant visa. Immigrants come in through the front door so to speak. For example, Arnold Schwarzenegger.

Polspeak: Any foreigner who enters the country, legally or illegally and regardless of if he intends to stay permanently. For example the person who sneaks across the border with the intent to work or sell the drugs he smuggled in, send money home, then return to his home country after acquiring sufficient funds for a good retirement there.

Investment

English: Using money or other resources to get a return, that return usually being more of the same type of resource invested. For example, a business may invest money in equipment that will manufacture an item to sell, thus getting back more money than was invested. Government may invest in sound education and thus reap the reward of more educated citizens who pay higher taxes and vote more wisely.

Polspeak: Taking citizens money or other resources for whatever the politician wants, or for whatever he thinks will buy votes in the next election. For example, taxing citizens in the entire country to build a bridge that is not needed but creates a few jobs in a particular congressional district. In Polspeak the purpose of an investment is either to get more votes or to increase the power of the politician.

Investigate

English: Trying to find the cause of a problem or otherwise understand that problem. This is usually done with an eye to solving or at least ameliorating the problem.

Polspeak Definition 1: Trying to find something to support what you already intend to do. For example seeking some evidence that a problem exists so you can spend money on that problem.

Polspeak Definition 2: Claiming you are seeking information and continuing to make that claim until enough time has passed that you can say that the issue is ancient history and no longer relevant.

Law

English: A fixed set of rules and consequences for violation thereof. It is important that the law be known beforehand and not changed to suit the situation. This fixed body of law allows citizens to govern their lives without fear that they will be declared criminals tomorrow on the basis of doing something that is legal today. The term "rule of law" means that the same laws apply to everyone from the garbage collector to the president, and that nobody can change the law except by the established process.

Polspeak Definition 1: What a judge or bureaucrat decides the law should say. By deciding on things like what words really mean, the decision maker can make the law say whatever he thinks it should say and apply it as he sees fit, retroactively if necessary.

Polspeak Definition 2: A body of rules applicable (under the conditions described in definition 1 above) to the masses. However different rules apply to celebrities of the right political persuasion, to government officials etc. The law can be easily bent to the advantage of such people.

Liberal

English definition 1: Someone who is generous with his or her own resources. For example a person who donates money or time freely to good causes and who helps others with their problems.

English definition 2: Someone who allows others to live their lives as they see fit. For example the person who says that he would never consider taking up a neighbor's hobby of sky diving, but the neighbor is free to do it since it does not harm others.

Polspeak definition 1: An advocate of big government controlling almost every aspect of life. This type of liberal may well want to outlaw risky sports such as skydiving for the good of the people.

Polspeak definition 2: Someone who advocates taxing the productive to provide for the non-productive with government controlled resources. The Polspeak liberal may even think ill of a person who gives freely of his own resources but opposes government forced "charity."

Liberty

English: The right of citizens to decide for themselves how they will live, subject only to minimal laws and not interfering unduly with the lives of others.

Polspeak: Government will provide what it decides people need and will have the liberty to do so. This includes determining how people should live.

Life

English: Living, those organisms that can grow and reproduce themselves. Also, living in such a manner as to enjoy life.

Polspeak: Opposition to abortion.

Limited Government

English: A restraint on government such that it cannot do certain things. For example government may be limited to not taxing one group more than others, or the power of the federal government may be limited to certain areas, leaving other issues to the states.

Polspeak: Huh? Limited government? What is that? Oh I get it. It is things we don't want the other party to do, but of course my party is good and should be allowed to do what it wants.

Living Wage

English: Not really defined since people have lived with so little throughout history that it is nearly impossible to determine what would be the minimum required to continue living.

Polspeak: Whatever wage a politician thinks will get him the votes required to win the next election. This definition is rather squishy since the living wage will increase as needed to support the politician's goals.

Meaningful Work

English: Work that earns a living and contributes to society. For example a plumber is doing meaningful work because he earns a living and contributes to clean water and waste management, enhancing life for those he serves. Even if a person hates his job, it is meaningful if it contributes to society.

Polspeak: Work that the person finds personally fulfilling. If a person hates his job it cannot be meaningful regardless of how useful it is to society. For example the above plumber is probably not doing meaningful work because he has to deal with sewer and other nasty stuff. However the artist is doing meaningful work even if nobody likes what he calls art.

Need

English: Something necessary to life, such as adequate food, shelter, or water. For example, we need a certain number of calories and other nutrients to remain healthy, so food in appropriate amounts can be considered a need.

Polspeak: Anything a politician can use to buy votes. For example, phone service claimed necessary for emergencies or job searching, but often used to talk to boyfriends or girlfriends.

Obstructionist

English: Someone who blocks a proposed action, law, etc. This can be either a valuable action or a detriment to progress depending on if the action or law is ultimately good or bad.

Polspeak: Anyone who opposes what we want to do, regardless of the reasons for that opposition.

Paperwork Reduction

English: Finding a way to reduce duplication and unnecessary paperwork. If less paperwork (including on-line forms not actually on paper) is required, paperwork has been reduced.

Polspeak Definition 1: Combining several forms into one horrendous form which demands twice the total information previously required,

Polspeak Definition 2: Eliminating one form and creating two new ones to document that paperwork has been reduced.

(Seeking) Peace

English: Doing what one believes is most likely to avoid war. That may include negotiation or deterrence, whichever is thought most likely to succeed. Indeed it often includes a combination, making potential enemies believe that they have nothing to gain by aggression while at the same time giving them enough that they can be at least somewhat satisfied and not feel threatened.

Polspeak: Disarmament and giving the potential enemy what he wants.

Personal Responsibility

English: A person is responsible for what he does with his life. For example, if he works hard he gains the reward of at least a decent income. If he goofs off or becomes addicted to drugs or alcohol, he is responsible for the consequences of his choice.

Polspeak: What? Personal responsibility? Such a thing cannot exist. Society or government is responsible for most outcomes. Big business is responsible for others as when they refuse to hire or promote people for trivial reasons such as lack of skills.

(Matter of) Principle

English: Bedrock belief, such as firm support of freedom. True matters of principle are few and their adherents will almost never change their support of those principles.

Polspeak: Whatever our side supports, especially if it will bring in votes. That could be freedom, or it could be the belief that certain groups should be given preference in education, jobs etc. These principles can change if that change will bring in more votes, as for example when certain politicians, once opposed to integration, started supporting civil rights laws.

Privileged

English: Someone born or married into wealth or power such as the Kennedys, John Kerry, or Al Gore

Polspeak: Anyone who has lots of money, especially if he earned it himself. However in Polspeak the Kennedys are not privileged since they support big government.

(The) Powerful

English: People with the ability to control others, often against their will. For example the bureaucrat who can order a farmer not to host a wedding on his farm. In English the most powerful entity is the government since it can control much of our lives.

Polspeak: Private enterprise or highly paid company officers. That applies even to businesses that cannot control customers. Even if customers can take their business to a competitor, the business leader will be considered powerful. However it does not include rich people such as John Kerry or the Kennedy family if they support your preferred politics. In Polspeak "the powerful" especially does not include anyone from government.

Progress

English: Something that helps solve a problem or provides a better life for most people. For example the development of a less expensive, more powerful computer. Another example would be the development of phone services that compete with each other, thus freeing people from the tyranny of telephone monopolies.

Polspeak: Something that increases the power of government and facilitates a return to the idea that government is all wise, as was believed in the days of kings. For example, a rule prohibiting farmers selling their produce directly to consumers. In Polspeak, creating monopolies is progressive if government controls those monopolies.

Progressive

English definition 1: Noun referring to someone who wants to improve something. For example, a company employee who suggests improvements in what that company does.

English definition 2: Adjective referring to ideas that improve things such as the ideas of the progressive employee. For example, an idea of how to reduce the cost of a product without harming its serviceability is a progressive idea. An educational change that helps students learn would be a progressive change.

Polspeak definition 1: An advocate of big government controlling almost every aspect of life.

Polspeak definition 2: Someone who advocates taxing the productive to provide for the non-productive with government resources.

(Note that in Polspeak "progressive" is synonymous with "liberal." This is convenient since self-proclaimed liberals or progressives can switch back and forth and call themselves whichever term is considered more acceptable at the moment.)

Promise

English: A firm commitment to do something. For example if an honest person promises to be at a certain place at a certain time, he will be there if reasonably possible – and before making that promise he will consider if he can really keep it.

Polspeak: Telling voters what they want to hear and helping them believe you really intend to do it. However, once the election is past, the word means nothing.

Public Interest

English: Something that attracts the interest of the public or is beneficial for most of the public. Examples would include entertainment that the public enjoys, or improving the economy so that more people can have jobs and support themselves.

Polspeak Definition 1: What powerful politicians think is good for the public or at least would get more votes for them. For example tax-funded "public interest" TV stations watched mainly by the people who want to get themselves on camera so they can think of themselves as TV personalities.

Polspeak Definition 2: Groups lobbying for their special interest, provided that the powers that be approve of that special interest.

Public Service

English: Serving the public, for example selling food at a reasonable price. If an enterprise meets public needs it is engaged in public service, be it government, private non-profit, or profit making. For example the Heritage Foundation is a public service organization since it attempts to educate people about government issues. Also, a company that hauls tons of food to market is serving the public since that public must eat.

Polspeak: Working for the government or in some cases a non-profit enterprise. For example, a bureaucrat who writes regulations that stifle private enterprise is engaged in public service. In Polspeak no profitable enterprise is considered public service, regardless of how effectively and efficiently it meets public needs and desires. Even a non-profit organization is not considered public interest unless that organization supports bigger government. The Heritage Foundation is not considered a public service organization since it opposes bigger government.

Quota

English: Any requirement that some person or organization have a particular number of some group as members, employees, in management positions etc. For example, a company may be required to have a certain percentage of Blacks in management. Government mandated quotas are usually enforced by legal action and calling them targets or goals does not change the fact that they are really quotas.

Polspeak: There is no such thing as a government set quota, only targets and goals. If people would only meet those targets and goals there would be no need for the legal action we must take when they fall short.

Return on Investment (ROI)

English: The measurable return on money or other resources invested. For example a business may invest $1000 in machinery. If that machinery improves profit by $5,000 the ROI is five times what was invested or 500%. In English, the ROI goes to the person or entity that provides the investment.

Polspeak definition 1: What? We never heard of such a thing! Once we invest tax money, that is the end of the matter. There is no reason to see if it actually accomplishes the supposed objective.

Polspeak definition 2: Oh wait, I get it. The ROI would be the number of votes my investment (as defined above for Polspeak) gets me next election.

Racism

English: Considering ethnicity in employment or other decisions. For example hiring, firing, or promoting a person or refusing to do so because of his skin color.

Polspeak definition 1: Failing to hire or promote the right number of people of a given skin color.

Polspeak definition 2: Failure to support big government spending programs.

Polspeak definition 3: Opposition to a minority politician, especially one with leftist or statist views. In this definition, the racist need not consider or mention the race of the person he opposes. The fact that he opposes a minority politician for any reason qualifies him as racist. However this does not apply to people who oppose minority politicians who support free markets and other "conservative" ideas (see the Polspeak definition for black men and women). Since in Polspeak black conservatives are not considered authentic Blacks, it is not racist to oppose them.

Racist (Nearly the same as bigot)

English: Someone who hates or discriminates against those of other races. For example the Ku Klux Klan, the boss who refuses to hire a black person, or the person who refuses to live near someone of a different race. This applies equally to people of all races. A Black who hates Whites is quite as racist as a White who hates Blacks.

Polspeak: Any political conservative. Anyone who opposes higher taxes or bigger government or who supports individual responsibility. However in Polspeak it is never racist to oppose a conservative or call him race-based names, regardless of his skin color. Also in Polspeak a black person can never be racist regardless of how prejudiced he is against those of other races.

Rehabilitation

English: Treating Criminals so that they do not re-offend. This may include long sentences in unpleasant places so that they do not want to return. It may also include teaching them work skills and to actually show up for work on time and put in a full day working. The measure of its effectiveness is lower recidivism.

Polspeak: Psychological counseling, classes etc. that claim to treat the root causes of crime. If the criminal has completed the course of therapy and classes he is considered rehabilitated.

Right

English definition 1: Something a person is entitled to, such as agreed upon pay for work done.

English definition 2: The conservative side of politics, especially those who prefer limited government. The terms go back to the National Assembly during the French Revolution when the supporters of the king sat on the right and the revolutionaries on the left of the assembly president. However today it has come to mean those who oppose growing government. That is a somewhat natural outgrowth of the original meaning. It comes from the time when left wanted change and the right wanted no change. Today most who want big government are asking for change. Those who oppose big government want to stop that change. Therefore the left is regarded as the big government supporters and the right is regarded as those opposing big government.

Polspeak definition 1: Something the government decides everybody, or people of a certain class should have, such as a cell phone that they do not have to pay for.

(Continued next page)

Polspeak definition 2: Anybody someone on the political left does not like. For example even though Stalin believed in unlimited government, many on the left want to claim that he was on the right. In Polspeak the political "right" includes groups as disparate as fascists and libertarians, groups that have essentially nothing in common. That is useful for slandering people but not for communicating real information.

Rights of the Accused

English: A body of rights provided to the accused in an effort to (1) safeguard against conviction of the innocent, and (2) prohibit cruel and unusual punishment. Since criminal justice is not a sporting event, there is no need to see that all of the accused have equal probability of escaping justice.

Polspeak: Making sure that criminals who are accused all have an equal chance to escape punishment. If an experienced criminal knows how to "beat the rap," we must make sure that less experienced criminals have the same advantage. Not to do so would be as unfair as having one sports team not know the rules.

Self-righteous

English: Thinking of oneself as better than others, especially a hypocrite. For example a mayor of Portland, Oregon who made a big deal of the fact that she didn't even own a car, thereby claiming that she was avoiding damage to the environment alleged to be caused by driving cars. Instead of driving her own car she had the police department chauffeur her around.

(Continued next page)

Polspeak: Anyone who urges people to live wisely and follow social standards and rules. For example those who point out that young women who become unmarried mothers often sentence themselves and their children to a life of poverty, and that their children will have a high risk of unpleasant encounters with the law. The fact that these people are telling the truth, and that their words would help prevent human misery is irrelevant.

Simplistic

English: Over simplifying something to the point that important aspects of the problem are ignored. For example, saying that education problems are solely the fault of the teachers, or solely the fault of parents.

Polspeak: Any argument you disagree with but cannot refute. (Note that this is not limited to the political arena.)

Society

English: A rather elastic term that refers to some collection of all the people. It may mean all the people in a state or country, or those who voluntarily associate because of a common interest such as the American Physical Society (a group of physicists). Society includes various types of people and is rather inclusive. However society as a whole is rather incapable of action. Only such societies as deliberately formed professional groups can act and be responsible for anything.

Polspeak: The root of all evil. If a person commits a crime, remains poor, or fails to get an education it has to be because society failed him.

Spending Reduction

English: Not spending as much as before. If a corporation spent a billion dollars last year, a spending reduction of 10% would mean that it will spend a hundred million less this year or only 900 million dollars. If that corporation instead spends 1.1 billion dollars, it would be called a 10% increase in spending.

Polspeak: Not spending as much as you initially propose. For example, if a government program spent a billion dollars last year, you might suggest spending 1.2 billion this year. Then you promise to cut spending so you only spend 1.1 billion. In Polspeak that is a spending reduction of 100 million dollars or almost 10%. Just ignore the fact that you are really spending 10% more than you did last year.

Solution

English: Some action or decision that solves a problem. A solution to uneducated children might be better teaching and strict expectations that the kids actually learn. In English the effectiveness of a solution is determined by results, that is if the problem actually gets solved. For example, do the children leave school better educated than before? What matters is reaching stated objectives.

Polspeak: Spending money or writing laws and regulations in the name of solving the problem. In Polspeak, the effectiveness of the solution is determined by how much money is spent or how many rules and regulations are imposed. What matters is the means, not reaching the objectives.

Special Interest Group

English: Any group promoting its own objective to the exclusion of what is good for the country in general. For example, a group demanding tax money to support its favorite drama club or a business group demanding protection from competition.

Polspeak: Any group trying to limit government power, for example the Tea Party. In Polspeak any group asking for an increase in government power is not a special interest group, it is a public interest group.

Statist

English: One who believes that government should control all or most aspects of life. This is similar to the Polspeak definitions of liberal and progressive.

Polspeak: The word does not exist in Polspeak since its use would be an admission of desire to control things beyond what the vast majority want.

Stereotype

English: Thinking of people as having characteristics of some group rather than as individuals. For example, believing that a Swiss immigrant is likely to be meticulous because the Swiss are known for that characteristic. Another example would be thinking that a Mexican must be a thief. A few stereotypes may hold true for most people from that group. However other stereotypes are completely wrong.

(Continued on the next page)

Polspeak: Similar to English with the following exceptions:

Criticism of someone you don't like is not considered stereotyping, even if the group does not at all fit that stereotype. For example, claiming that Tea Party members are automatically racist is not considered stereotyping even though evidence for the claim is lacking.

It is automatically stereotyping if someone you like is criticized. For example, if someone criticizes Barrack Obama for a political position, they are stereotyping him as a black man, even though the criticism has nothing to do with his skin color.

Stigma

English: Some indication that a person is not acceptable to others. This may be either deserved or undeserved. An undeserved stigma would be something like bias against people of a certain skin color. On the other hand, a person who refuses to bathe will stigmatize himself by making himself stinky and unpleasant to be around. A person who refuses to work for a living may suffer the deserved stigma of being considered a leech on the productive.

Polspeak: Characterization of anyone except the people we don't like, always unfair. For example thinking ill of welfare recipients or promiscuous single mothers. However thinking ill of our political enemies is never stigmatizing, they deserve it.

Subsistance

English: The absolute minimum required to maintain life, especially the minimum food or weather protection to sustain human life. If a person does not acquire that minimum, death will follow.

Polspeak: Whatever we decide is the minimum required for a good life, usually depending on how many votes that amount of largesse will bring our candidate. This may include enough to acquire a big-screen TV, a pack a day smoking habit, air conditioning, the latest style of athletic shoes etc.

Success

English: Reaching a defined objective, for example reducing violent crime in certain places by 10%. Such success must be measured by looking at how things change, with the measurement done the same way before and after the solution is applied. The measure of success is the ends achieved, not the means used to reach those ends.

Polspeak Definition 1: Putting in place laws or regulations claimed to be related to the problem, for example putting up signs that certain places are gun-free zones. Once that is done it would be silly to see if violent crime actually declines in those zones. The measure of success is the means applied to the problem.

Polspeak Definition 2: Modifying statistical measurements to make them look better For example a jurisdiction might institute a policy of not arresting people for certain crimes and thus reduce the measured crime rate in that jurisdiction.

Target (See the entry for "goal.")

Temporary

English: Something that will not last long. For example a temporary barrier around a construction site. Once the construction is complete and there is no longer a need, the barrier will be removed.

Polspeak: A word used to get around public opposition to a proposed tax, law, or rule by leading people to think that it will not be in effect very long. In fact there is really no need for a temporary program to end soon, or even ever. For example, there was a "temporary" excise tax on telephones established in 1898 to help fund the Spanish-American War. Unlike many temporary measures, that one was repealed – in 2006.

Tolerance

English: Allowing others their beliefs and opinions even when those beliefs and opinions contradict what you are convinced is the truth. Often includes the recognition that you might learn from those who disagree with you.

Polspeak definition 1: Agreeing to allow others their beliefs and opinions as long as either they are quiet about it, or those beliefs and opinions agree with your own.

Polspeak definition 2: Being completely non-judgmental about which of two similar things is better. For example, insisting that *War and Peace* is no better literature than is a comic book, or that single parenthood is as good as a two parent home.

Violence

English: Use of physical force to harm a person, animal or property. For example beating someone with fists or some other object, or shooting him with a firearm.

Polspeak: Any failure to provide selected people with what we think they should have, such as the failure to give decent housing to people who do not earn that housing. For example it is considered economic violence if someone opposes more food stamps.

Women's Health

English: Keeping women and girls healthy. Includes avoiding health problems by vaccination, nutrition, and sanitation, care to avoid accidents, cancer screening and treatment, dealing with menopause, osteoporosis, cardiovascular problems, and in fact all aspects of health for women and girls. Reproductive health is part, but only part, of women's health.

Polspeak: Abortion and contraception.